3D BAND BOOK

A THREE-DIMENSIONAL APPROACH TO A BETTER BAND
As easy as ONE-TWO-THREE!
BY JAMES D. PLOYHAR & GEORGE B. ZEPP

CONTENTS

TO THE STUDENT

The 3-D BAND BOOK is a three-dimensional approach to REHEARSAL PREPARATION. This complete TUNE UP-WARM UP program will *reduce rehearsal stress* and *permit greater accomplishment* with *less effort*. The overall preparedness that this book provides will make every rehearsal a more rewarding and enjoyable experience.

The book is divided into the following sections:

I. TUNE UP-WARM UP

II. KEY PREPARATION

III. RHYTHM PREPARATION

In addition, there are three pages of HARMONY and EAR TRAINING which will provide the basic knowledge necessary for relating to the EXERCISES and CHORALES found in the book. By following the instructions as to the use of this book, as explained by your director, you will be able to approach every rehearsal period with confidence and skill.

CHORALES

PUBLISHED FOR:

Conductor	B♭ Bass Clarinet	E♭ Baritone Saxophone	Baritone (Treble Clef)
Flute	Oboe	B♭ Cornet-Trumpet	Baritone (Bass Clef)
E♭ Clarinet	Bassoon	Horn in F	Bass (Tuba)
B♭ Clarinet	E♭ Alto Saxophone	Horn in E♭ (Mellophone)	Drums
E♭ Alto Clarinet	B♭ Tenor Saxophone	Trombone	Bells

Introduction to HARMONY

HARMONY IS THE ART OF COMBINING NOTES INTO CHORDS. IT IS THE STUDY OF HOW THE ELEMENTS OF MUSIC ARE PUT TOGETHER.

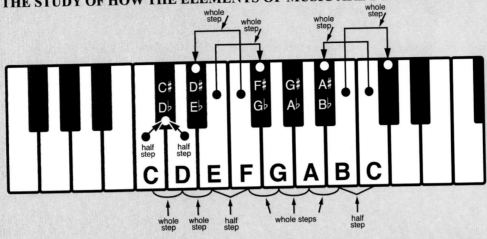

On the piano keyboard pictured above you can see that a HALF STEP is the distance from one note to the note directly above or below it, regardless of whether it is a black key or a white key. Notice that E to F and B to C are half-steps because there is no black key (half-step) between them. A WHOLE STEP consists of TWO half-steps.

Intervals

AN INTERVAL IS THE DIFFERENCE IN PITCH BETWEEN TWO NOTES

Intervals are identified by numbers. The number name of an interval tells you how much higher its top note is than its lower note.

To find the number name of an interval, count the lines and spaces between the notes. Count the bottom note as "one." The number of the top note tells you the name of the interval.

STUDY THE FOLLOWING EXAMPLES:

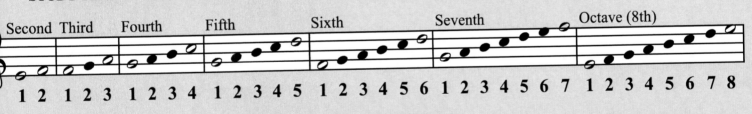

Major and Minor

Intervals also have SIZE names. The size of an interval is determined by the number of STEPS and HALF-STEPS between the two notes

Some intervals (2nd, 3rd, 6th, 7th) can be MAJOR (large) or MINOR (small). FOR EXAMPLE:

The notes of a MAJOR (large) 3rd are TWO WHOLE STEPS apart:

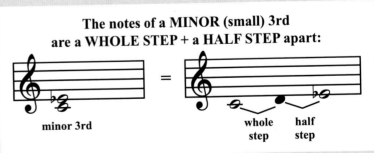

The notes of a MINOR (small) 3rd are a WHOLE STEP + a HALF STEP apart:

The following intervals are thirds. You decide if they are major or minor by counting steps and half-steps. The keyboard picture at the top of the page will tell you which notes are only a half-step apart.

MEMORIZE: The intervals that can be MAJOR or MINOR are the 2nd, 3rd, 6th, 7th.

Perfect Intervals

The intervals that are not major or minor are PERFECT. They are the prime, fourth, fifth, and octave.
A PRIME is the interval of "one." It is made by two instruments sounding the same note. An OCTAVE is the interval of an "eighth."

> A fifth on any note of the staff (without flats or sharps) is PERFECT.
> EXCEPTION: The fifth from B to F is diminished.
> A fourth on any note of the staff (without flats or sharps) is PERFECT.
> EXCEPTION: The fourth from F to B is augmented.

Augmented Intervals

A PERFECT interval made larger becomes an AUGMENTED interval.

A perfect interval may be made larger by RAISING the TOP note a half-step:

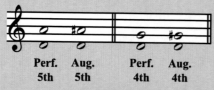

or by LOWERING the BOTTOM note a half-step:

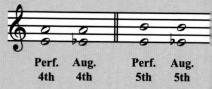

Diminished Intervals

A PERFECT interval made smaller becomes a DIMINISHED interval.

A perfect interval may be made smaller by LOWER-ING the TOP note a half-step:

or by RAISING the BOTTOM note a half-step:

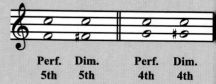

Chords

A CHORD IS A GROUP OF NOTES WHICH BLEND HARMONIOUSLY WHEN SOUNDED TOGETHER.

The simplest chord consists of three notes. It is called a TRIAD.

A chord or triad takes its name from the note upon which it is built. That note is called the ROOT of the triad:

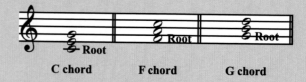

The note above the root is called the THIRD of the triad. It makes an interval of a 3rd above the root:

The note above that is called the 5th of the triad. It is a 5th above the root:

There are four kinds of triads:

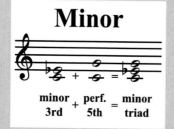

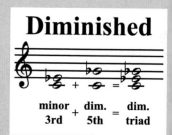

Chord Symbols

In addition to its letter name a chord or triad has a number. Its number is the step of the scale on which the chord is built.

For example, C is the first note of the scale in the key of C. The chord built on C will therefore be the "one" chord in that key. It is identified by the Roman numeral I.

A capital letter means the chord is major. A small letter means the chord is minor. The VII chord is diminished. Here are the letter and number names of chords in the key of C:

Musical examples on this page may be played by the entire band.

Introduction to

EAR TRAINING

It will be helpful to you to know the THEORY of music as it is written; but it is even more important to learn to HEAR harmony.

Here are some intervals that you will hear often in your music. Continue to review this exercise until you can recognize them by their sound. Listen for them as you play the chorales in this book.

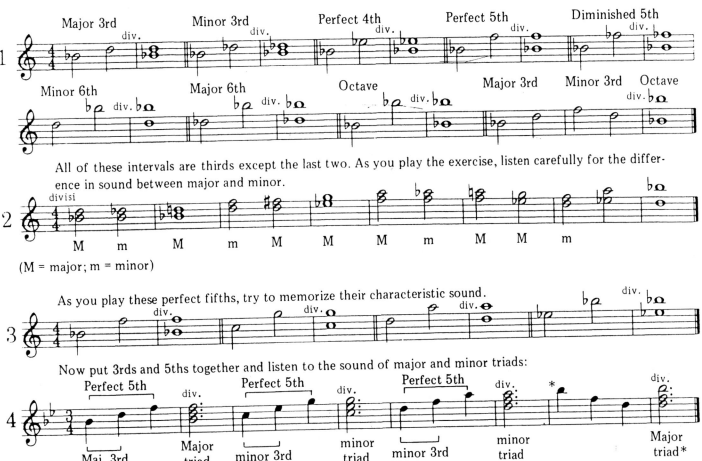

All of these intervals are thirds except the last two. As you play the exercise, listen carefully for the difference in sound between major and minor.

(M = major; m = minor)

* Inverted (upside down) triad with the root on top.

The Principal Chords

The principal chords in any key are the I, the IV, and the V.
The I chord is called the TONIC chord. The V chord is called the DOMINANT chord.
The IV chord is called the SUBDOMINANT, because it is below the dominant.
SUB means UNDER or BELOW.
EVERY NOTE OF THE SCALE CAN BE HARMONIZED USING THESE THREE CHORDS

Principal Chords In Major

Principal Chords In Minor

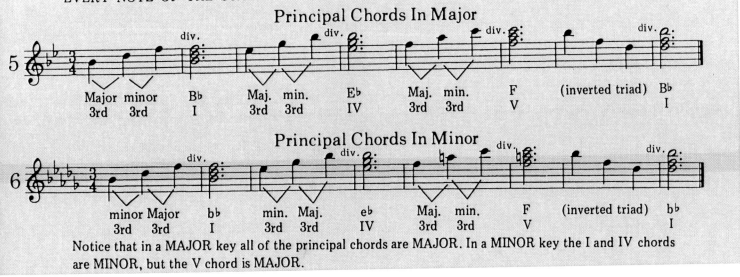

Notice that in a MAJOR key all of the principal chords are MAJOR. In a MINOR key the I and IV chords are MINOR, but the V chord is MAJOR.

I. Tune Up - Warm Up

For tuning purposes the band is divided into four basic groups. Group I includes Flutes, Piccolos, Oboes, Eb Clarinets and Bb Soprano Clarinets.

UNISON TUNING is accomplished by utilizing measures 1 and 2 of each line. A reliable instrument or tuning device should be used to tune the instruments in Group IV. Other groups are then added to this unison.

The tendency of the note to be *flat* or *sharp* is indicated by a symbol to the right of the note. Students should adjust pitches accordingly. The Arabic numerals to the left of the note indicate the note's position within the chord.

Lip Slurs
(Brasses)

8

Embouchure Studies
(Woodwinds)

G. Parès

Dominant Seventh Arpeggios
(Woodwinds)

EL. 2859

Chromatic Exercise

For best results the band should play the entire page without stopping. However, the conductor may choose to rehearse one or more lines of chromatic scales that are appropriate to the rehearsal piece. Apply various articulations to these scales.

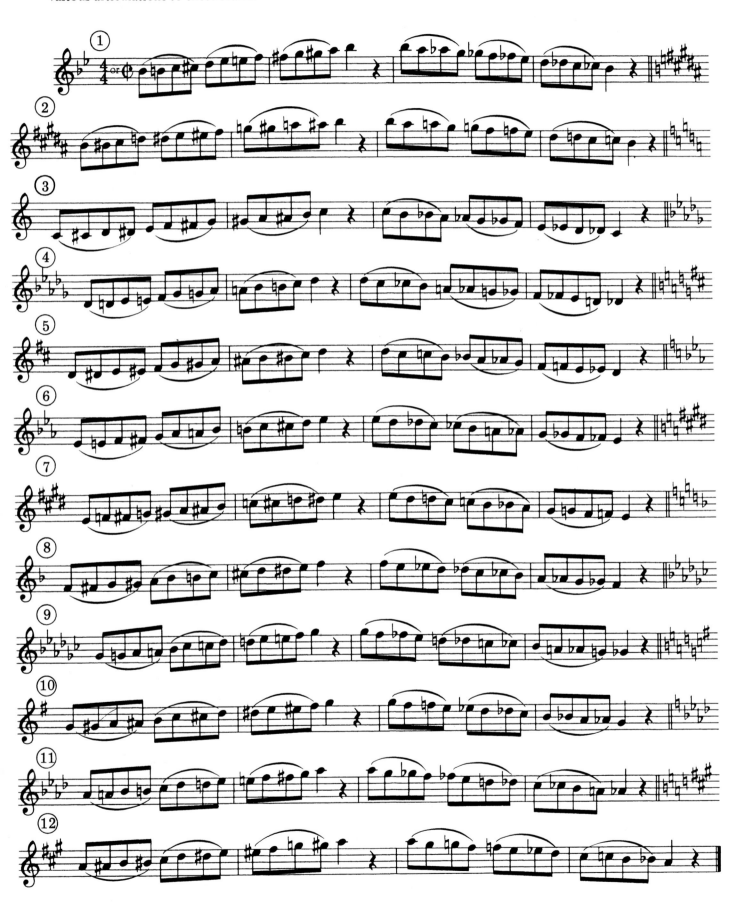

II. Key Preparation
Key of B♭ Major

Scale in Half Notes

1

Harmony

2

Scale in Eighth Notes

3

Scale in Thirds

4

Scale Skills

5

Principal chords in the key of B♭ Major. Try to identify them in the chorale.

6

A Mighty Fortress Is Our God

M. Luther
Arranged by J.S. Bach

7

[A]

Key of G Minor

Scale in Half Notes

1

Harmony

2

Scale in Eighth Notes (Harmonic Form)

3

Scale in Eighth Notes (Melodic Form)

4

Scale Skills

Ployhar

5

Principal chords in the key of G Minor. Try to identify them in the chorale.

6

When On The Cross The Saviour Hung

J.S.Bach

7

Key of E♭ Major

Scale in Half Notes

1

Harmony

2

Scale in Eighth Notes

3

Scale in Thirds

4

Scale Skills

5

Principal chords in the key of E♭ Major. Try to identify them in the chorale.

6

How Brightly Shines The Morning Star

P. Nicolai
arranged by J.S. Bach

7

[A]

Key of C Minor

Scale in Half Notes

1

Harmony

2

Scale in Eighth Notes (Harmonic Form)

3

Scale in Eighth Notes (Melodic Form)

4

Scale Skills

5

Principal chords in the key of C Minor. Try to identify them in the chorale.

6

Jesus, Priceless Treasure

J.S. Bach

7

Key of F Major

Scale in Half Notes

1

Harmony

2

Scale in Eighth Notes

3

Scale in Thirds

4

Scale Skills

5

Principal chords in the key of F Major. Try to identify them in the chorale.

6

Let All Together Praise Our God

J.S. Bach

7

Key of D Minor

Scale in Half Notes

1

Harmony

2

Scale in Eighth Notes (Harmonic Form)

3

Scale in Eighth Notes (Melodic Form)

4

Scale Skills

5

6

Principal chords in the key of D Minor. Try to identify them in the chorale.

Who Is The Man?

German Melody

7

16

Key of A♭ Major

O Thou Of God The Father

J.S. Bach

EL. 2859

Key of F Minor

Scale in Half Notes

1

Harmony

2

Scale in Eighth Notes (Harmonic Form)

3

Scale in Eighth Notes (Melodic Form)

4

Scale Skills

5

Principal chords in the key of F Minor. Try to identify them in the chorale.

6

The God Of Abraham Praise

Hebrew Melody

7

Key of C Major

Scale in Half Notes

1

Harmony

2

Scale in Eighth Notes

3

Scale in Thirds

4

Scale Skills

(in 2)

5

Principal chords in the key of C Major. Try to identify them in the chorale.

6   div. I   div. IV   div. V   div. I

The Blessed Christ Is Risen Today

Praetorius

7

Key of A Minor

Principal chords in the key of A Minor. Try to identify them in the chorale.

Lord God, Now Open Wide Thy Heaven

M. Altenburg

Key of D♭ Major

Scale in Half Notes

1

Harmony

2

Scale in Eighth Notes

3

Scale in Thirds

4

Scale Skills

5

6

Principal chords in the key of D♭ Major. Try to identify them in the chorale.

Watchman, Tell Us Of The Night

J.S. Bach

7

[A]

Key of B♭ Minor

Come, Let Us All With Fervour

J.S. Bach

Key of G♭ Major

Scale in Half Notes

1

Harmony

2

Scale in Eighth Notes

3

Scale in Thirds

4

Scale Skills

5

Principal chords in the key of G♭ Major. Try to identify them in the chorale.

6

I   IV   V   I

To God We Render Thanks And Praise

M. von Hessen

7

Key of E♭ Minor

Scale in Half Notes

1

Harmony

2

Scale in Eighth Notes (Harmonic Form)

3

Scale in Eighth Notes (Melodic Form)

4

Scale Skills

Moderato (in 2)

5

Principal chords in the key of E♭ Minor. Try to identify them in the chorale. *rit.*

6

In Peace And Joy I Now Depart

J.S. Bach

7

Key of G Major

Scale in Half Notes

1

Harmony

2

Scale in Eighth Notes

3

Scale in Thirds

4

Scale Skills

5

Principal chords in the key of G Major. Try to identify them in the chorale.

6

Hark! A Voice Saith, All Are Mortal

J.S. Bach

7

[A]

Key of E Minor

Key of D Major

Scale in Half Notes

Harmony

Scale in Eighth Notes

Scale in Thirds

Scale Skills

Kopprasch

Principal chords in the key of D Major. Try to identify them in the chorale.

O God, In Whom We Live And Move

Johann Schein

Key of B Minor

Scale in Half Notes

1

Harmony

2

Scale in Eighth Notes (Harmonic Form)

3

Scale in Eighth Notes (Melodic Form)

4

Scale Skills

5

Principal chords in the key of B Minor. Try to identify them in the chorale.

6

O Sacred Head Now Wounded

Hans Leo Hassler

7

Key of A Major

Scale in Half Notes

1

Harmony

2

Scale in Eighth Notes

3

Scale in Thirds

4

Scale Skills

5

Principal chords in the key of A Major. Try to identify them in the chorale.

6

The Beauteous Day Now Closeth

Heinrich Isaak

7

[A]

Key of F♯ Minor

Scale in Half Notes

1

Harmony

2

Scale in Eighth Notes (Harmonic Form)

3

Scale in Eighth Notes (Melodic Form)

4

Scale Skills

5

rit.

Principal chords in the key of F♯ Minor. Try to identify them in the chorale.

6

Come, Christian Folk

J.S. Bach

7

III. Rhythm Preparation

The conductor will select one or more measures from the following rhythms that are appropriate to the rehearsal piece. Play each measure (or measures) on every tone of a given scale.

Each of the next eight pages contains two *unison* RHYTHM STUDIES. Practice each study separately. Then, for an added challenge, divide the band or class into two groups. Half the band plays the top study while the other half plays the bottom study. You may also practice them as DUETS with other students.

Eighths and Sixteenths

Rhythm Study

Rhythm Study

Alla Breve
(Cut Time)

Three Eight Time

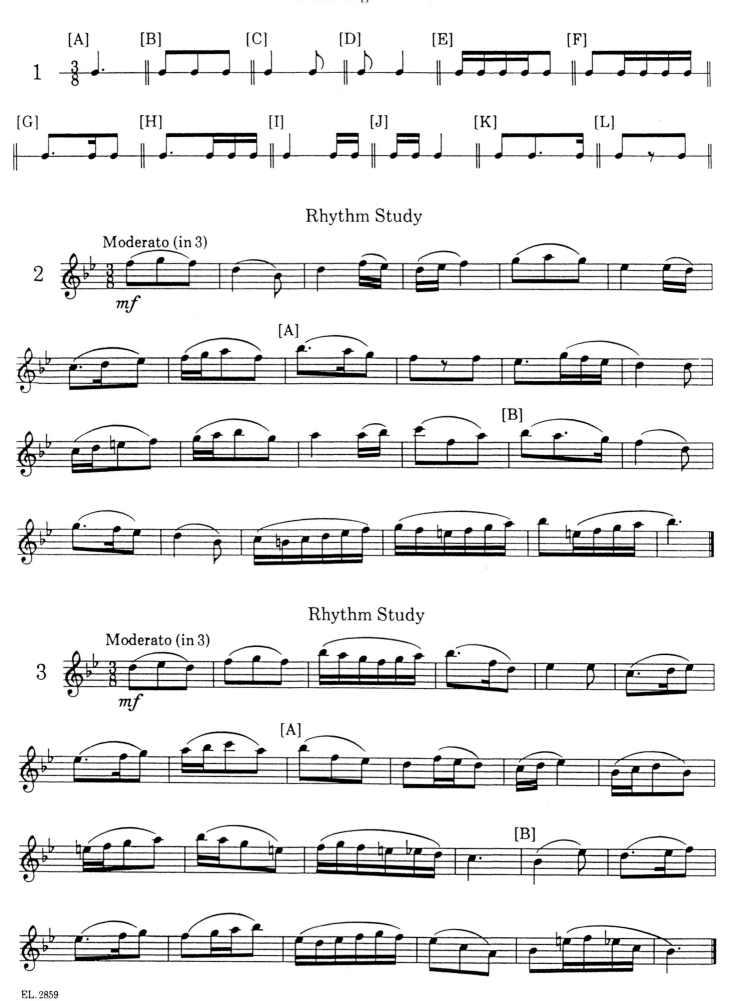

Rhythm Study

Rhythm Study

Six Eight Time

Rhythm Study

Rhythm Study

Triplets

Rhythm Study

Rhythm Study

Nine Eight Time

Rhythm Study

Rhythm Study

Mixed Meters

In much of the music of the 20th century a change in the TIME SIGNATURE or METER may also require a change in the BEAT or PULSE. In the following example the duration or value of the eighth-note remains the same. The conductor will normally give ONE BEAT (pulse) to the $\frac{3}{8}$ measure, but the duration of the beat (pulse) will be one eighth-note longer than the regular beat (pulse) of the $\frac{4}{4}$ measure or the $\frac{2}{4}$ measure. THE $\frac{3}{8}$ MEASURE REQUIRES AN *IRREGULAR* BEAT OR PULSE.

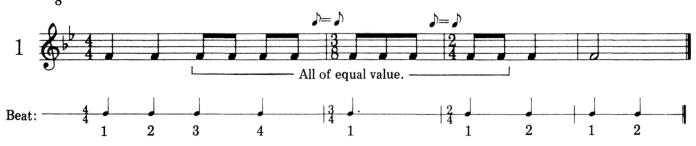

Rhythm Study

In the following example the duration or value of the eighth-note remains the same. The conductor will normally give TWO BEATS (pulses) to the $\frac{5}{8}$ measure. Two eighth-notes will receive a *regular beat* (pulse) and three eighth-notes will receive an *irregular beat* (pulse) which is one eighth-note longer in duration.

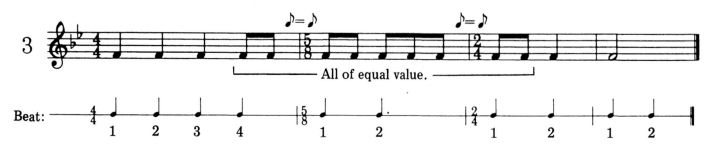

Rhythm Study

In the following example the conductor will normally give THREE BEATS (pulses) to the $\frac{7}{8}$ measure. Four eighth-notes will receive *two regular beats* (pulses) and three eighth-notes will receive an *irregular beat* (pulse) which is one eighth-note longer in duration.

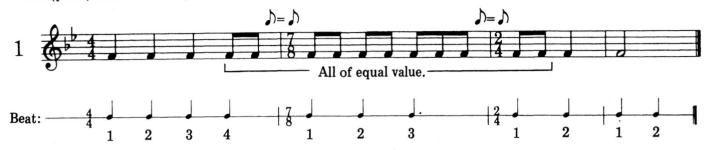

Rhythm Study

In the following example the duration or value of the sixteenth-note remains the same. The conductor will normally give ONE BEAT (pulse) to the $\frac{3}{16}$ measure, but the duration of the beat (pulse) will be one sixteenth-note shorter than the regular beat (pulse) of the $\frac{4}{4}$ measure or the $\frac{2}{4}$ measure. The $\frac{3}{16}$ measure requires an *irregular* beat or pulse.

Rhythm Study

In the following example the duration or value of the sixteenth-note remains the same. The conductor will normally give ONE BEAT (pulse) to the $\frac{5}{16}$ measure, but the duration of the beat (pulse) will be one sixteenth-note longer than the regular beat (pulse) of the $\frac{4}{4}$ measure or the $\frac{2}{4}$ measure. The $\frac{5}{16}$ measure requires an irregular beat or pulse.

Rhythm Study

In the following example the duration or value of the sixteenth-note remains the same. The conductor will normally give TWO BEATS (pulses) to the $\frac{7}{16}$ measure. The four sixteenth-notes that are beamed together will receive a regular beat, but the three sixteenth-notes that are beamed together will receive a beat or pulse that is one sixteenth-note shorter than the regular beat.

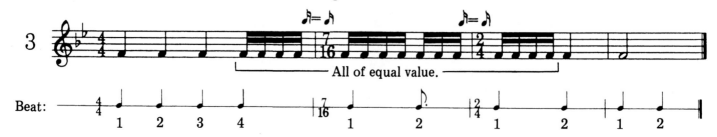

Rhythm Study